WIDE OPEN SPACES

ISBN 0-634-00286-4

HAL•LEONARD®
CORPORATION

7777 W. BLUEMOUND RD. P.O. BOX 13819 MILWAUKEE, WI 53213

Visit Hal Leonard Online at
www.halleonard.com

CONTENTS

I CAN LOVE YOU BETTER

Words and Music by PAMELA BROWN HAYES
and KOSTAS

WIDE OPEN SPACES

Words and Music by
SUSAN GIBSON

As her folks drive a-way, her dad yells, "Check the oil."

Mom stares out the win-dow and says, "I'm leav-in' my girl." She said, "It

LOVING ARMS

Words and Music by
TOM JANS

if I could on - ly hold you now. ___ I've been

too long in ___ the wind, ___ too long in ___ the rain, ___

tak - in' an - y com - fort ___ that I can. ___

Look - in' back ___ and long - in' for ___ the free - dom of ___ my chains ___

THERE'S YOUR TROUBLE

Words and Music by TIA SILLERS
and MARK SELBY

YOU WERE MINE

Written by MARTIE SEIDEL
and EMILY ERWIN

NEVER SAY DIE

Words and Music by RADNEY FOSTER
and GEORGE DUCAS

will nev - er say die.

TONIGHT THE HEARTACHE'S ON ME

Words and Music by MARY FRANCIS,
JOHN MacRAE and BOB MORRISON

44

But to - night the heart - ache's __ on __ me, _____ on __ me, __

yeah. Let's __ drink a toast __ to the fool _____ who could - n't see. __

LET 'ER RIP

Words and Music by BILLY CRAIN
and SANDY RAMOS

48

ONCE YOU'VE LOVED SOMEBODY

Words and Music by THOM McHUGH
and BRUCE MILLER

I'LL TAKE CARE OF YOU

Words and Music by
JOHN DAVID SOUTHER

Original key: B major. This edition has been transposed up one half-step to be more playable.

AM I THE ONLY ONE
(WHO'S EVER FELT THIS WAY)

Words and Music by
MARIA McKEE

Solo ends   Now my __ sense of hu - mor needs __ a break. __

GIVE IT UP OR LET ME GO

Words and Music by
BONNIE RAITT

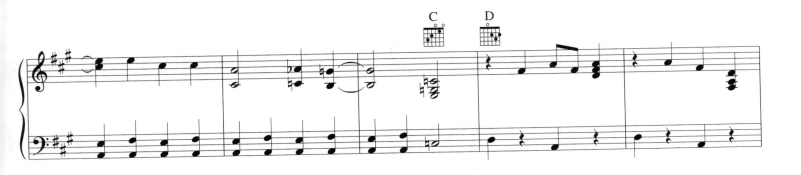

74

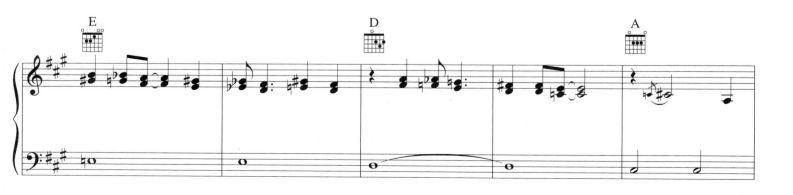

Instrumental solo

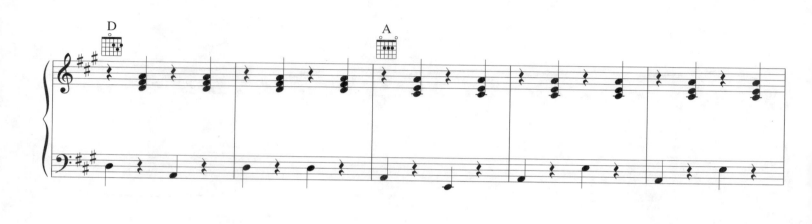